# GET RICH QUICK!

# GET RICH QUICK!

Les Karamazov

PAPERMAC

First published 1988 by
PAPERMAC
a division of Macmillan Publishers Limited
4 Little Essex Street London WC2R 3LF
and Basingstoke

Associated companies in Auckland, Delhi, Dublin, Gaborone, Hamburg, Harare, Hong Kong, Johannesburg, Kuala Lumpur, Lagos, Manzini, Melbourne, Mexico City, Nairobi, New York, Singapore and Tokyo

ISBN 0–333–48520–3

Typeset by Wyvern Typesetting Limited, Bristol
Printed in Great Britain by
Mackays of Chatham PLC, Chatham, Kent

*Some of the ideas mentioned in this book might be construed as an incitement to break the spirit if not the letter of the law. It is not the intention of the publishers, the author or distributors in any way to recommend that people get found out.*

*Introduction*

# HOW TO MAKE £1,000,000 in 27 Days

You've probably always promised yourself that ONE day you're going to sit down and make that million. But you've just been too busy working to really concentrate on it; too busy to notice that time is slipping away and that if you're not careful you will NEVER be

Paul Getty
Robert Maxwell
Richard Branson
Aristotle Onassis
Elton John
Midas

But at last there's a way to make a million without spending a lifetime sweating over it. You CAN make enough money never to have to work again – and all in just 27 days!!

By the ingenious application of rudimentary mathematics, Professor Les Karamazov has discovered that by simply taking one penny – yes, 1p – and doubling it every day for 27 days you can become a MILLIONAIRE!!! Just look at these figures:

| | |
|---|---|
| Day 1 | 1p becomes 2p |
| Day 2 | 2p becomes 4p |
| Day 3 | 4p becomes 8p |
| Day 4 | 8p becomes 16p |
| Day 5 | 16p becomes 32p |
| Day 6 | 32p becomes 64p |
| Day 7 | 64p becomes £1.28 |
| Day 8 | £1.28 becomes £2.56 |
| Day 9 | £2.56 becomes £5.12 |
| Day 10 | £5.12 becomes £10.24 |
| Day 11 | £10.24 becomes £20.48 |
| Day 12 | £20.48 becomes £40.96 |
| Day 13 | £40.96 becomes £81.92 |
| Day 14 | £81.92 becomes £163.84 |
| Day 15 | £163.84 becomes £327.68 |
| Day 16 | £327.68 becomes £655.36 |
| Day 17 | £655.36 becomes £1,310.72 |
| Day 18 | £1,310.72 becomes £2,621.44 |
| Day 19 | £2,621.44 becomes £5,242.88 |
| Day 20 | £5,242.88 becomes £10,485.76 |
| Day 21 | £10,485.76 becomes £20,971.52 |
| Day 22 | £20,971.52 becomes £41,943.04 |
| Day 23 | £41,943.04 becomes £83,886.08 |
| Day 24 | £83,886.08 becomes £167,772.16 |
| Day 25 | £167,772.16 becomes £335,544.32 |
| Day 26 | £335,544.32 becomes £671,088.64 |
| Day 27 | £671,088.64 becomes £1,342,177.28 |

## *It's Easy*

Of course if it was that easy to make money we'd all be millionaires, wouldn't we? But contrary to general belief you do not have to be a financial whizz-kid to make a fortune. Very often the first penny is the most difficult – so I've given it to you. Off you go – and Good Luck!!

# THE KARAMAZOV BUSINESS PLAN

The now famous Karamazov Business Plan has been developed over a period of twenty years, during which time I have been amongst the most successful entrepreneurs in SE5. Previously these investment strategies have been available only to those willing to buy the author the odd pint at the Dick and Duck but now for the first time it is possible to buy the complete set of plans in one comprehensive book.

Each day's plan has been carefully constructed and fully tested to double the available capital. While every effort has been made to simplify the plans they do still require commitment, dedication and sometimes a little preparation on your part. But if you are prepared to work hard and follow this book to the letter you will soon be £1,000,000 better off!!

*Les Karamazov at his desk.*

**The Free Suit**

Go to the library and get a copy of *Who's Who*. Find the address and phone number of a quite-but-not-too-famous person. Ring up and announce that Madame Tussauds is commissioning a waxwork of them and you need to arrange a sitting. After consulting the diary also mention that you will be dropping round to collect a typical suit of clothes and perhaps even some personal effects for the completed model.

# DAY ONE

## 1p TO 2p

*The Fountain of Life*

Making your first penny can be one of the most rewarding of life's experiences. You will look back on the day you first doubled your money with affection and a certain sadness – those were the days. In fact this *is* the day, so make the most of it.

Our first day's strategy is a simple scam but has a certain elegance to it. I first came across it in 1951 when in Rome trying to sell Cornish icecream – it seemed a good idea at the time but after four hours it had all melted and I was left with nothing but a polythene bag full of pale yellow liquid. It was in this hour of desperation that I invented the Fountain of Life.

1. Find a fountain in a busy public place. If possible this should be old and battered.

2. Look wonderingly at the water then take out your penny, press it against your forehead, murmur a prayer and toss it in.

3. Walk away with a confident smile.

4. Wait until someone else follows suit and then retrieve both pennies. If no-one takes up the cue, simply collect your penny and start again.

# DAY TWO

## 2p TO 4p

*Spending a Penny*

You have now broken the most important psychological barrier – you have proved to yourself that it is possible to double your money. Although it may seem a small beginning – after all, two pence is hardly going to buy you the flat in Lanzarote – the major hurdle has been overcome. It is now simply a matter of taking the bit between your teeth and going on to double and double until you reach the magic one million pounds.

Two whole pennies – a little wet perhaps but they are yours. The next investment is to be in the public service. It is so easy that many ex-pupils have christened it a piece of piss.

1. Find a decent class of public lavatory – perhaps in a hotel or fancy restaurant.

2. Wedge all the cubicle doors shut with toilet paper.

3. Wait until someone comes in and then start dancing about. Say you need two pence more for the loo and offer to buy them for ten pounds, to write a cheque, to sign over your house – 98% of punters will willingly give the money for nothing. The other two may suggest some other sort of deal which you may or may not wish to take up depending on your mood.

## The Free Breakfast

Although in less than a month you will be able to afford to buy an entire chain of restaurants, in these early days it will be difficult to get enough to eat from day to day. However, with a little ingenuity you need never be short of a bite.

Walk into a large hotel, go up to the reception and ask if a Mr Hofstader has checked in yet. While the receptionist checks, scan the key rack and note a couple of rooms which are occupied. Then thank the receptionist and ask if it's all right if you wait.

Find an in-house telephone and call room service. Order a large meal for one of the rooms you noted but ask that it be left outside the door as your child is ill and can't be disturbed.

Wait a few minutes and then go up to the room to collect your meal. Try to find either a spare room, lavatory or cupboard where you can eat it in peace.

*Take just one penny . . .*

## What do you do if you Lose Your Penny

If you really are such a klutz that you can't even hold on to ONE FREE PENNY, do you really think that you are going to make it through this course? However, just in case it was not completely your fault (quite what could happen that wasn't your fault is beyond me though) I will give you a second chance.

If you have absolutely nothing, your entrepreneurial possibilities are limited to begging, borrowing or stealing. What with high interest rates and heavy prison sentences you are for all practical purposes reduced to begging – not an attractive option for a potential millionaire but then you can't be a chooser, can you?

The basic tenet of successful begging is to appear nonchalant and not too needy. The same principle applies to begging as it does to selling, namely the punter's response: 'If you're selling I don't want to buy.' Thanks to thousands of years of civilisation and the evolution of social conscience most people's attitude remains, 'If you need it I'm not going to give it to you.'

However, the opposite also remains true, namely, 'If you don't need it I will give it to you.' This attractive quirk in human nature is called the Karamazov Window of Begging Opportunity. To take advantage of it you must appear smart, tidy, well-spoken and, above all, rich. If you fulfil these requirements people will be delighted to hand out charity. What they can't stand is giving alms to those who deserve it.

Approach anyone in the street with something along the following lines: 'Excuse me, this is really embarrassing but I've got to buy my wife some flowers and, it's really stupid I know, but I'm just one pee short. I know this sounds awful, but I don't suppose you could possibly . . . ?' Very, very few people will refuse you. Indeed most, going through their change and finding they have only a five or ten pee piece will give you that. You are already well on your way!

# DAY THREE

## 4p TO 8p

*Busking without an Instrument*

Busking has always been an excellent way to make a few pounds on the side. All one needs is an instrument of some kind, a little talent and the gall to ask the public for money. Unfortunately you are unlikely to have either the instrument or the talent – however, you do have the gall so not all is lost.

Busking without an instrument may at first seem difficult if not impossible, until you remember one of the fundamental principles of capitalism and the basis of Karamazov's Second Law.

1. Make yourself a hat from an old cardboard box.

2. Find a busker with a large crowd. Put your four pence in the hat as 'seed money'.

3. Work your way through the crowd shaking the hat and looking people straight in the eye. Most will be far too embarrassed not to pay something. If the busker should notice, you simply smile and point to the money – he will be very reluctant to stop and it will probably not even cross his mind that you are about to proceed to the final stage:

4. Run away.

# KARAMAZOV'S SECOND LAW OF MAKING A PACKET

*'Let other people do the work.'*

*This boy is talented.*

# DAY FOUR

## 8p TO 16p

*Organising Tours*

Today's objective, to double your money from eight to sixteen pence, should not take more than a couple of hours at the most. However, you may wish to spend longer at it since not only can it double your money but it can also increase your social life by a factor of ten.

The idea is to arrange sightseeing tours. At first this may sound rather grandiose – 8p will not exactly hire a coach or pay for a professional guide – but do not be daunted, the secret here is authenticity.

1. Find a monument or building that looks old but is not particularly well known. It is no good going for St Paul's or the Tower of London, but neither is there much mileage in a plaque celebrating an unknown poet somewhere in East Dulwich. Choose somewhere on the tourist route but not already covered by books or other guides.

2. Dress accordingly. If, for instance, it is a London pub you have chosen, dress as a Pearly King or Queen – you do not have to go all the way, just the odd button to give a general impression will do. If in the country, try tying bits of ribbon round your legs and banging some sticks together. None of this need cost very much. Below is one of the costumes I have used.

*. . . and this car park is over 150 years old.*

3. Stand by your chosen monument. As soon as a group of tourists goes by at least one will have to ask you what you are doing there. You can then spin a lengthy story about how your family has always been connected to the place, ever since the first stone was laid. Don't forget to add that the most famous member of your family emigrated shortly after the monument was built and went to make his fortune in America, Canada, Australia or wherever your audience comes from.

4. You will now have a captive audience. Spin them as many yarns as possible, the more absurd the better. They will be spellbound and afterwards, despite your earnest pleas not to be paid, they will slip you a little something.

If they don't – ask.

*It's for a weally good cause!*

## This Week's Good Cause

Wash out some old baked bean cans, tie on some string and wrap labels round them printed with 'This Week's Good Cause'. Go up to the first person you meet in a crowded street and say, 'You look like an honest person. Could you hold this for five minutes – I've got to go to the loo. Perhaps you'll do better than me!' Repeat, till you have used up all your cans. Then go round and relieve your first 'helper' who should have collected about 50p. Pocket the money and start again. Repeat all day. It's a nice trusting touch to hand the 'helper' a half filled can. But it is a bitter reflection on the degenerate morals of our present society that you can't really trust anyone these days so perhaps it's better to fill it with old bits of metal just in case.

# DAY FIVE

## 16p TO 32p

*The Peaked Cap*

In these early days, and with just 16p to spare, it may seem exorbitant to start spending money on equipment, but today you will learn how to make one of the most useful items of your career: the peaked cap.

### Instructions

You will need a piece of shiny black card, some cloth or paper, some cardboard, glue and scissors. First measure your head and add two inches – no official wears a cap of the right size, one of the characteristics of the authentic peaked cap being that it is always too large. Copy a heraldic device onto the front. This cap has been specially developed to lend authority; the Latin motto 'Conus ergo Sum' translates as 'I con therefore I am'.

### How to Use your Cap

This simple accessory will earn you many times its original cost. It is quite amazing, and for you profitable, to note the respect for authority that 99% of the population have. When I hear politicians and bishops complain about public morals and discipline I feel like shouting at them: 'WEAR A PEAKED CAP!' I myself have walked from one end of the 7.28 from East Croydon to the other collecting excess fares from every old lady on the train, armed with nothing more than a peaked cap and a pair of nail clippers. This is an easy operation requiring you to do little more than scowl and ask for money.

There are any number of business opportunities open to you now you have your cap, as the following photographs show:

*That's £2.00 for the packet and £4.75 for the cigarettes.*

*Sorry, EEC regulations: £12.50*

# Postman's Knock

Day 1: Wait till you see the postman coming down the street. Stand by a front door as if you were just leaving the house. Say 'Good Morning, Postman' and go off down the road.

Day 2: Repeat.

Day 3: Repeat but as he comes up to put the letters in the door you are by, say 'Good Morning, Postman – oh – I'll take those.'

Day 4: Wait till he's gone. Doff your cap, take out a scruffy notebook full of addresses and signatures and ring the bell. When a bleary-eyed punter opens it, announce cheerily; 'Special Delivery – £1.45 excess please, looks like rain, sign here please, thank you, hope it keeps clear, good morning.' Please note: failure to repeat bland statements about the weather/ state of the nation/life in general may jeopardise your disguise.

*Special delivery*

# DAY SIX

## 32p TO 64p

*The Milk of Human Kindness*

For this ingenious scheme I am indebted to G. K. Chesterton who wrote of it in one of his 'Father Brown' stories. He explained how an enterprising crook started a milk round with the minimum of investment. First he enlisted new customers by calling on them, engaging them in charming banter and explaining that he could supply delivered milk at a cut rate. He then persuaded them that if they wished to take advantage of his offer they would have to pay in advance. This done, bright and early each morning he simply switched the milk from other people's doorsteps to those of his own customers.

Obviously the Karamazov student has a good deal to learn from this example. It is a clean, simple and effective venture. The only investment needed is a milk rack, a couple of old milk bottles and, that old favourite, a peaked hat. The secret of the enterprise is to persuade the punter they are getting a good deal and saving money.

## KARAMAZOV PRINCIPLE NO. 3

'People will part with large sums of money if they think they are going to save a few pence.'

*Don't arouse . . . suspicion.*

**The Free Car**

Getting a free car is not as difficult as it may appear, especially if all you want to do is impress someone for the afternoon. Dress as smartly as possible, go along to the most expensive car showroom you can find and ask what the delivery is like on the Jaguar. Get talking; the salesman will sooner or later suggest a trial run. Resist. Hum and haw. Eventually arrange for him to pick you up at your house (wherever the scene of your next business venture is) *et voilà* – a car and chauffeur.

# DAY SEVEN

## 64p TO £1.28

*Getting into the Property Market*

Everyone knows that the real money over the last twenty years or so has been made in property. There is a limited amount of space and an ever increasing number of people wanting it. It is the perfect economic model – supply is constantly outstripped by demand.

However, you may feel that day 7 is a little early to enter this very profitable business. Admittedly most property developers start off with more than 64p but this should not deter you. There is a way into the property market without laying out huge sums of money.

### Letting

The secret of successful letting is twofold – first, you do not have to own what you let, secondly start small. The Karamazov Letting Plan is simple: you sell car parking space.

1. Make sure your 64p contains six 10p pieces.

2. Choose a metered area in the busiest part of London – say Covent Garden or Oxford Street.

3. Get up early one morning (when there are plenty of free meters) and put your money in the meter. Lie down in the space. Wait for an hour and a half. The

traffic will now be pretty busy. Drivers will start to hoot and yell at you to get out of the way.

4. You can now ask a driver how much he is willing to pay you to leave. At first he may turn abusive but when you point out that you have paid your money and nowhere does it say you have to park a car there, he may begin to see your point. Especially if there are three other cars behind him hooting.

5. This is your opportunity to initiate an auction. You will find that people are willing to pay quite a high premium just to get hold of your space. Once you have the highest bidder, take the money, vacate the space and move on to another.

In this way you will soon double your money and perhaps also make some lasting friendships.

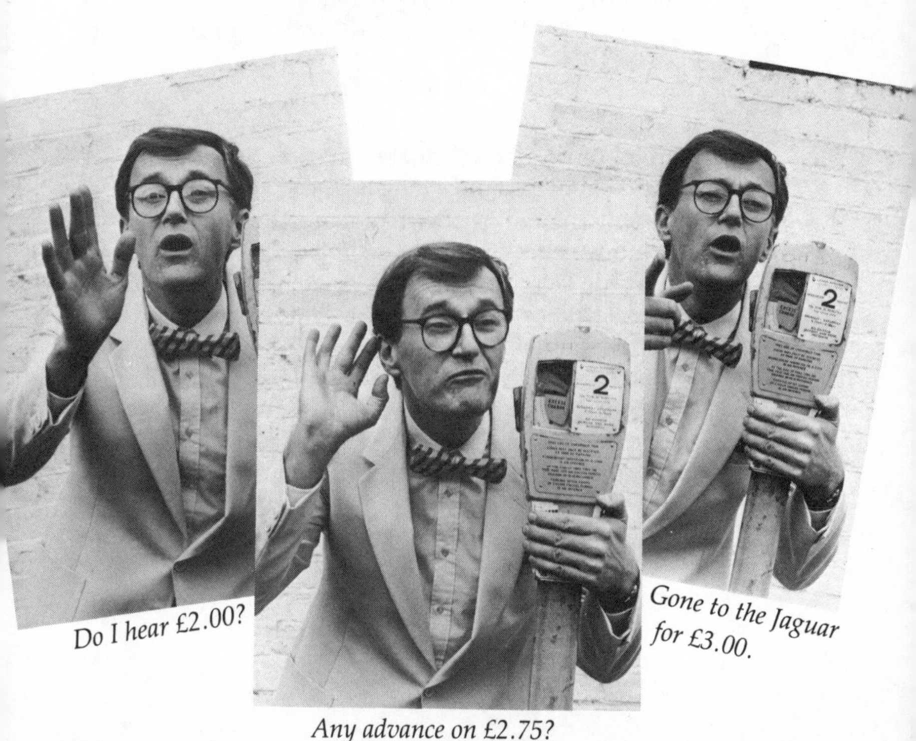

*Do I hear £2.00?*

*Any advance on £2.75?*

*Gone to the Jaguar for £3.00.*

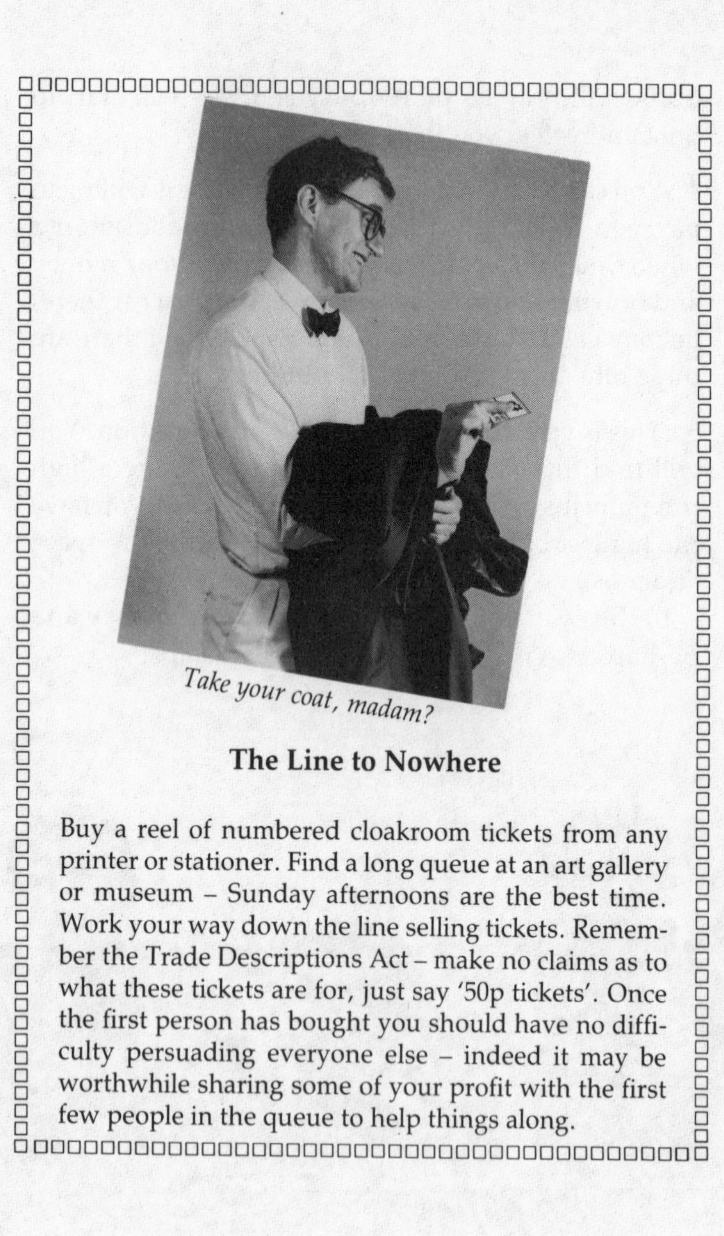

*Take your coat, madam?*

## The Line to Nowhere

Buy a reel of numbered cloakroom tickets from any printer or stationer. Find a long queue at an art gallery or museum – Sunday afternoons are the best time. Work your way down the line selling tickets. Remember the Trade Descriptions Act – make no claims as to what these tickets are for, just say '50p tickets'. Once the first person has bought you should have no difficulty persuading everyone else – indeed it may be worthwhile sharing some of your profit with the first few people in the queue to help things along.

# DAY EIGHT

## £1.28 TO £2.56

*Dearly Beloved*

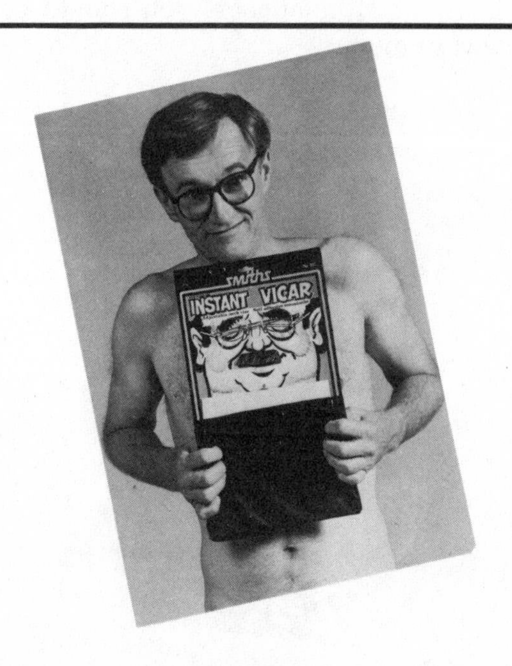


You now have £1.28 and can afford to make some serious capital investment. You will need to buy:

1. A small wooden bowl
2. A stiff collar
3. A long black piece of material

Wrap the material round your body and put the collar on back to front. You should now look like the picture below:

Go to the nearest church on Sunday at about 11.00 a.m. Put your change in the bowl and, very discreetly, pass it up and down the pews. I remember the time when this ruse would provide enough ready cash for a jolly good booze-up but even in these days of immorality and profaneness you should be able to double your money.

*Please give generously.*

**Why Didn't I Think of That?**

If you shampoo and vacuum your carpet, why not your hair? I see a definite market niche for a reverse hair-dryer that vacuums out the dandruff.

# DAY NINE

## £2.56 TO £5.12

*Selling Newspapers*

You may feel that by this stage being a newspaper vendor is beneath you. After all, it is now day 9 and you already have over two pounds. But there has always been money in newspapers – just look at Beaverbrook, Murdoch and Maxwell.

They all knew that what sells newspapers is stories – good, sensational stories topped by incredible headlines such as VICAR EATS BABY DURING SERMON. This will be the secret of your success.

1. Go to a newsagent and ask for any leftover papers from the day before. Say you are collecting them for a Blue Peter charity and he will be only too pleased to let you have as many as you can carry.

2. Invest in a stencil and a tin each of white and black spray paint.

3. Spray white paint over the old headlines. Then stencil in your own headlines. The rule is that nothing can be too shocking or unbelievable – the more totally ridiculous the headline the more people will want to read the story. Here are some examples that have worked for me in the past:

MOTHER GIVES BIRTH TO OWN TWIN
I WAS RAPED BY A UFO
WATCHING TV CAUSES CANCER

4. Set yourself up at a station during the rush hour. People will see the headline, buy the paper and run to catch their train. By the time they realise that a) the headline bears no connection to the story and b) it is yesterday's paper anyway, they will be a safe couple of miles away. In a few hours you should be able to sell all your papers and make a large profit. You may even cause other papers to pick up on your story.

## On the Road

Place this ad in a local paper:

**Have Fun! Meet People! Go on Mystery Tours!**

*If you are bored, retired, at home with nothing to do or simply want to have a bit of an adventure, then Uncle Les's Party Surprise Club is for you. Join the club and you'll never know what's going to happen next! One day it's a visit to a film set, the next it's a play or an artist's studio. You never know who you'll meet or what that crazy Uncle Les will suddenly ask you to do. It's fun all the way.*

At £3.00 to £5.00 an hour there is a surprising demand for bodies who will just sit and be themselves. I once sold twenty-two OAPs to a film company as extras for a remake of Tarzan. At the end of the day I couldn't get them out of their gorilla suits to come back home, they were having such a time! Artists' models are much in demand too. If you get fed up simply hire your members out to the Medical Research Council.

# DAY TEN

## £5.12 TO £10.24

*Working for Charity*

Go into a large stationery shop such as Rymans or Smiths and, pretending to try out the typewriters, copy the following:

| Name | Address | Amount per mile | TOTAL |
|---|---|---|---|
| | | | |
| | | | |
| | | | |
| | | | |
| | | | |
| | | | |
| | | | |
| | | | |
| | | | |
| | | | |
| | | | |

Take your sheet of paper and have it photocopied twenty or more times. Now fill in the first few lines as follows:

Colonel Portway-Fletcher, 38 The Mews, Chelsea, £2.00
Mrs J. Anderson, 18 Park View, Balham, £1.00
etc., etc.

You are now ready to approach your first sponsor. Choose someone whom you know something about. For example, follow people home from the tennis club. You can then tell them you are going to attempt to play tennis for twenty-four hours without stopping. With a bit of luck they will not ask who the money is going to, but if they do, be truthful – The Organisation for Youth in Tennis or whatever your age and recreational inclinations dictate.

A few days later you can return looking suitably exhausted and collect your money.

*Forty-nine miles.*

# DAY ELEVEN

## £10.24 TO £20.48

*The Big Chief Clerk*

I'm sure you'll all agree with me that traffic congestion is the bane of our cities and towns. I'm sure that you will also know that the cost of pursuing traffic offenders is a major problem – the authorities just can't afford all those police, traffic wardens and so on. Here is your chance to make some money and perform a socially useful act.

Temporarily borrow a parking ticket from the windscreen of a car. Substituting your address at the bottom where it says 'Chief Clerk of the ...... Council', take the ticket to an instant print shop and run off some few hundred of your own. Stick the original ticket back on the car and off you go – a freelance traffic warden.

*Remove the ticket discreetly.*

You'll soon find the good areas around town and it may be possible, with a little imagination, for you to break new ground in the automobile congestion field. Why should control be limited to the highways – what's wrong with controlling parking in people's front drives? How about ticketing a traffic jam?

Very soon the cheques will come flooding in. However, before you start to gloat, you must go down to your local bank and open an account in the name of a visiting Indian chief from Arizona – perhaps he wants to invest monies from land settlements in the stable UK market. This story will enable you to establish an account in the name of Chief Clerk.

**The Free Sausage**

Get out your felt tip and make a sign saying 'VEGETARIAN CUISINE'. Stick it up outside a greasy spoon café. Wait for a vegetarian to go in. Whatever he or she orders they'll get sausage, egg and chips. Then nip over to their table, apologise profusely and remove the offending sausage.

## Looking the Part

As a dynamic and successful business person it is important to create the correct impression. This often means appearing to be more successful than you really are – especially at the beginning of your career when you have only one penny to rub together. However, by careful planning it is possible to give the appearance of great wealth and importance without actually having it.

There are two main methods of achieving this: Faking and Borrowing. In the first category come such things as the phoney phone – a plastic eau de Cologne box that looks just like a car phone but in fact does nothing at all; or a kid's squeaky rubber duck which you keep hidden in your pocket and bleep to summon you to a phone when you want to get out of a meeting. The second is to borrow. For example you can borrow an expensive suit/car/partner from a friend or perhaps from a rather unobservant shop, for the afternoon.

*Hi!*

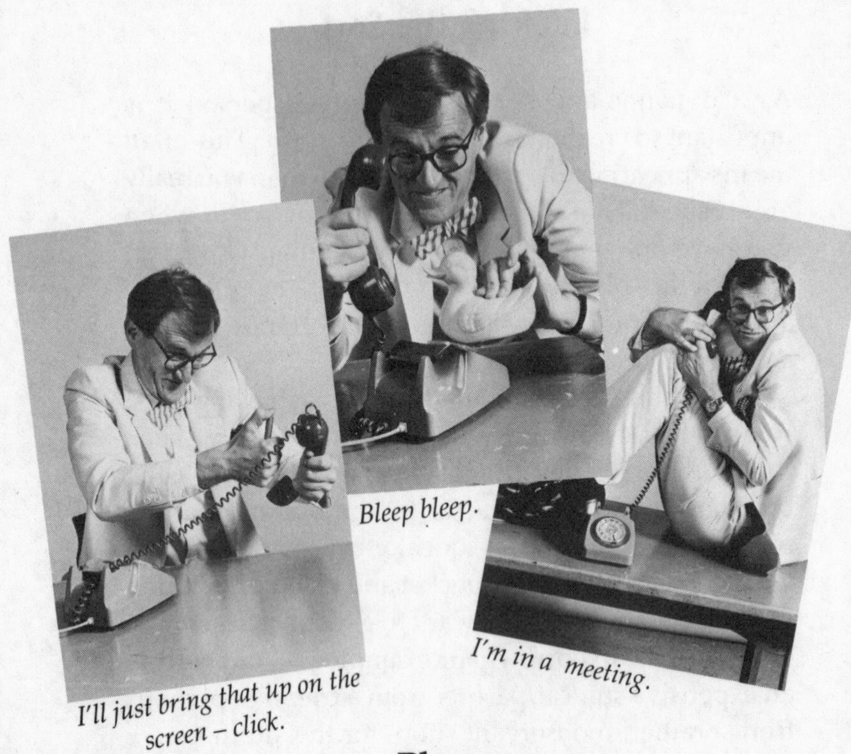

*I'll just bring that up on the screen – click.*

*Bleep bleep.*

*I'm in a meeting.*

## Phones

The phone is the most important tool of modern business. Not only does it facilitate fast, efficient communication but it also says a lot about how successful you are. It is therefore vital that you develop the correct telephone manner when talking to punters.

1. Have a tape recording of office noises which you can play in the background, thus giving the impression you are phoning from your hectic corporate headquarters.

*I'm afraid he's busy right now.*

*I'm speaking from the car.*

2. Buy a cheap retractable biro and click it so it sounds like a computer terminal. Say things like 'I'll just bring those figures up on the screen,' click click click.

3. When on a payphone make interference noises – static, buzzes, screeches, etc. – so that people think you are using a portable phone.

4. Every now and again interrupt callers saying, 'Hold on a minute, there's a call on one of the other lines.'

## How to Cheat with your CV

**Name:**

The name is important. It must not sound too common, such as Fred Jones, nor too posh, such as The Honourable Hilary Heffington-Smythe. Names that give an air of authority are Quatermaine, Jamieson, Kingsway and so on. Do not use fashionable or trendy names such as Fez or Silkin. Nicknames, along the lines of Basher Higgins, are not really recommended.

**Address:**

Always use a London address. People who live outside London are rarely taken seriously. Very exclusive areas, such as Park Lane or Holland Park are clearly forwarding addresses. Go for places where you could live but which are neither too fashionable nor too poor.

**OK areas:**

Battersea, Wandsworth, Balham, Clapham, Islington, Notting Hill, Fulham, Barnes.

**Not OK:**

Brixton, Mile End, Hackney, Docklands, Mayfair, Covent Garden, Bond Street.

**Age:**

You are always in your early thirties.

**Experience:** This is one of the most important parts of your CV. Of course you will claim experience in the field you are trying for, but it is also wise to include other activities. People are impressed by leadership skills, initiative and the bizarre. It is therefore a good idea to throw in a few Amazonian expeditions and perhaps some VSO in Bhutan.

**Education:** You were educated abroad. This not only makes you more exotic but makes tracing exam results almost impossible. Any of the Scandinavian countries are a good bet, as are Yugoslavia and Turkey. However, beware smart-arses who might suddenly ask you a question in Serbo-Croat. You attended university and have at least three degrees, though the exact nature of your PhD is difficult to ascertain.

**Hobbies:** The secret is not to sound too ostentatious. While skiing and hang-gliding are fine on their own, together they make you out to be a superman. Of course you spend a good deal of your time helping the disabled.

**References:** See under References.

# References

Whether it be to convince a bank manager, punter or prospective employer, a good reference will always oil the wheels. Naturally you will write these yourself but there are certain points to bear in mind.

1. The better the paper the more convincing the reference. Obviously a testimonial written on loo paper will not go down as well as one on the best Basildon Bond. The easiest way to lend credibility to your references is to use headed notepaper. This is simple to obtain: just pop down to your local printers, say you are setting up a new business and ask for samples of their letterheads to show your partner. They will willingly give you a wide selection of the best quality letterheads they do.

2. Type your reference. If you do not have access to a typewriter go into a large stationers such as Smiths or Rymans and, pretending to try out the machines, type what you need.

3. Be credible. It is often tempting to go over the top when composing your own references, saying such things as 'Mr Karamazov is simply the best business brain I have ever come across' or 'there has not been such an all-rounder since Leonardo'. Temper your enthusiasm with a little reality – while singing your praises suggest that the company is slightly bitter about you leaving and that you were, perhaps, too good for them. It's not a bad idea to throw in some small defects, too, such as 'tends to work too hard' or 'at times seems only to live for his job'.

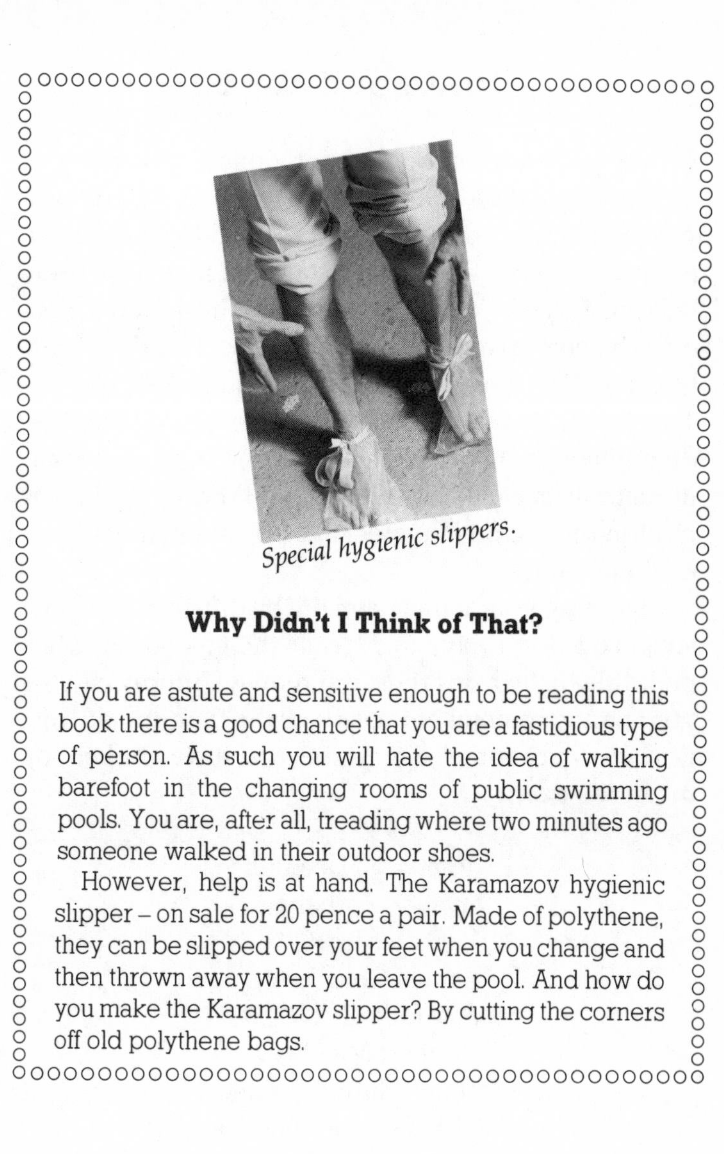

*Special hygienic slippers.*

## Why Didn't I Think of That?

If you are astute and sensitive enough to be reading this book there is a good chance that you are a fastidious type of person. As such you will hate the idea of walking barefoot in the changing rooms of public swimming pools. You are, after all, treading where two minutes ago someone walked in their outdoor shoes.

However, help is at hand. The Karamazov hygienic slipper – on sale for 20 pence a pair. Made of polythene, they can be slipped over your feet when you change and then thrown away when you leave the pool. And how do you make the Karamazov slipper? By cutting the corners off old polythene bags.

## The Correct Name

Before you can seriously contemplate becoming a millionaire you need to adopt a name that sounds as if you are already one. Now you may feel that your own name is perfectly adequate, in fact you may have been looking forward to all the people who ignored you over the years reading about your success and wishing they hadn't sneered at your Marks and Sparks anorak. This is just pride and must be overcome. Millionaires do not have ordinary names. There are no memorable industrialists called Jim Smith, no Fred Jones runs a multi-national; millionaires, like pop stars, must have credible names.

Changing your name need not be difficult or expensive. You don't have to register the change by deed poll, this just wastes time and money. Simply choose your name, remember to use it all the time and off you go. Below are some suggestions that have worked for me in the past:

Zachary Daedalus
Chuck Zorbanger
Cecilia Pi
James Gold Smith
Aristotle O. Nassis
Robert Max Well
Jeremy Minthenswaite
Patricia Portway-Fletcher

## The Correct Signature

Once you have hit upon your name it is important to practise the signature. As we all know, writing is a clear sign of character. A potential millionaire with the correct name but the wrong signature handicaps himself unnecessarily. Your new signature should be bold, decisive and confident. Below are some examples you can copy and others you should avoid.

# DAY TWELVE

## £20.48 TO £40.96

*Cashing In*

£20.48 may not sound like a great deal and a million may still seem a long way off but just think, you have already made a 2,000% profit in just 12 days!!

Although it may be tempting to go out and splurge at this stage – perhaps on a cup of tea and a small cake – try to resist this. It is better to be hungry now rather than poor later.

Take your £20.00 and go to a scrap metal yard. There you should be able to pick up an old cash till for about £15.00. If you drive a hard bargain you might even have some change for a cup of coffee.

With the remaining £5.00 buy as many plain brown paper bags as possible.

Take your cash till home, clean it and cover with a large towel.

Now go to a big store at a really busy time – Harrods sale would do nicely or Marks and Spencers just before Christmas. Find a suitable table, and set your till down. Soon people will be bringing things to you. All you have to do is pop them in the paper bags and take the money. After a few minutes you will have easily doubled your money.

*Merry Christmas and a Happy New Year.*

## Christmas – a Time for Giving

Early one morning go to a row of houses with dustbins at the front. Take the lids off them all and throw them in the street. Take the contents of one dustbin and empty it over the front steps of each of the houses. Now go to each one in turn and ring the bell saying 'Merry Christmas from your Garbage Disposal Team' and hold out your hand. The Institute record is £250.00 an hour – see if you can better it.

# DAY THIRTEEN

## £40.96 TO £81.92

*The Karamazov Express Courier Service*
*Motto: Here Today, Gone Tomorrow*

The enterprising Karamazov student must always keep pace with modern developments and fashions if he or she is to take advantage of them. A case in point is the recent obsession with speed. Everything now must be done twice as fast as it was yesterday. Where people used to send letters they now send couriers, where they used to send couriers they send faxes. If fast is good, faster is better. This offers enormous potential.

You may feel that £40.96 is a little on the small side to get into the courier business. True, a fleet of powerful motorbikes and greasy kamikaze riders can add up to more than the price of a good meal, but once again ingenuity can surmount all problems.

The secret here is that in a business obsessed with speed and delivery times people tend not to pay too much attention to formalities such as signing chits, checking identities or even paying over cash.

Buy a large, full-face crash helmet, a tatty, greasy, patched jacket and a pair of worn-out leather gloves. Now go into any big office around five thirty, when everyone is desperate to go home. Head for reception and, without removing your helmet, say something like 'Courier, package for mumble mumble.' Now this 'mumble mumble' is very important – on its credibility lies the success of the whole operation. It must not sound specific enough to be questioned, nor must it sound so incomprehensible as to give the game away. If you hit it just right the receptionist will, with luck, hand over a package.

Once you have the package, hold out a damp, crumpled, oil-stained piece of paper for them to sign, at the same time mumbling, '£8.20, please.' The receptionist will probably respond with something like 'Wot!' or 'We've had an account with you for ten years!'

*Sign here, luv.*

You then go on to explain: 'New rules. Don't blame me. Bad payers, isn't it? Look, love, there's fifteen cops crawling round my bike out there – you wouldn't want to hold this urgent packet up, would you now? Give us the money – I'll give you a receipt and you can get it back from petty cash. OK?'

You then take the money and on your way home pop the package in the nearest letterbox. Repeat this same ruse ten times and you will have achieved your target for the day.

## The Dry Well

The airlines have saved millions by changing the little bottles their miniature liqueurs and whiskies come in from glass to plastic, thus reducing their weight problem. You can help them overcome this further with lightweight instant mineral water.

Read the side of a Perrier or Evian mineral water bottle – it tells you all about the trace elements and minerals in it. Now go and buy these from a chemist; I think you'll be amazed at how cheap they are and how much you get. Then put them in little bags with a label saying:

INSTANT DEHYDRATED MINERAL WATER
ALL THE GOODNESS, NONE OF THE WEIGHT

*(Just add water)*

# DAY FOURTEEN

## £81.92 TO £163.84

*Cleaning Up*

You now have £81.92 – enough to make a small investment in your next scheme.

For this you need to buy a bucket, a sponge, a variety of rags and two very long pieces of strong rope.

1. Find the tallest office building you can and take the lift to the top floor.

2. Go out onto the roof and attach your pieces of rope about twenty feet apart. Then throw them over the side so that they dangle in front of the windows.

3. Go into each office and say something along the lines of 'Mr Clean, £26.50.' Most people will unthinkingly dip into the petty cash.

## Note

The success of this particular scam depends entirely upon your ability to look and speak exactly like a real window cleaner.

*Appearance*

Old tee-shirt with sweat stains, preferably cut at

shoulders to reveal bulging muscles.

Tattoo on right bicep. This can be inked in with a biro and should say something like 'Maureen' or 'I love Mum'.

Baggy, ripped jeans. These should be worn halfway down the hips to reveal as much bum-crack as possible.

Ripped trainers.

## *Speech*

Restrict your speech to things like ''allo darlin', you can wring my sponge any time' and 'Wor, look at the bazookas on that.'

*'s'tenner*

# DAY FIFTEEN

## £163.84 TO £327.68

*Nanny Knows Best*

Kiddies? Don't you love 'em – bless their little hearts. But, as every parent knows, they are a bit wearing in the holidays. Most of my admirers know that I am an avid supporter of the feminist movement especially when it comes to helping Mother out by looking after the nippers.

You will need £150 worth of cheap chocolate bars and a few bottles of tomato sauce; a couple of hundred cheapo leaflets; an old frock and a pudding basin hat.

This is what you do. First, prepare a leaflet something along the lines below and stuff it through the letterboxes of a nice middle-class neighbourhood.

*Come here, little boy.*

**CRECHE**

*– Supervised Play Mornings*

Trained Nanny has places for a few more under sixes at fully supervised play mornings. Licensed local premises; collection and return by arrangement. Please bring teddies, wellies and warm clothing. Lunch extra. Phone Mrs X on ......

Next you sit by the phone. While you wait, you could type yourself out a few glowing references. When the phone rings, say sorry you are now full up. Ten minutes later call back and say, delight of delights, that you have had a cancellation for tomorrow – would little Rasputin like to come along and try it out? Next morning you put on the frock and hat and go round to collect them all.

Any parent will tell you that what interests kids most are other kids, making a mess, chocolate and tomato ketchup. I think that most play schools tend to forget that these days – it's all Suzuki, Monty Sawrey, *Peter and David Live Together*, etc. What the little beasts want is a good fight, a lot of old junk to smash up and chocolate. So that is what you give 'em. Find a builder's skip in the road; get a long ladder; drop the little chickadees into the skip and let them get on with it. They'll have the time of their lives. Any tears and you just buzz a bar of chocolate down. Any hunger pangs and you buzz the ketchup down. End of the morning you chuck a bucket of water over the lot of 'em to wash the filth away. Just say little Histeria had a wee accident, but we aren't going to embarrass her by talking about it, are we? No probs.

Two things might go wrong. First, the builder may want his skip back – in which case slip him a fiver and take the brats on a quick jog to the next one. Secondly, and rather more dangerously, the bambini may have had such a wonderful day that their parents will plague you to death with imploring phone calls for a repeat. Unless you want to do this for the rest of your life, be prepared to make your phone number unlisted. We have bigger fish to fry tomorrow!

**Why Didn't I Think of That?**

The trouble with tea bags is that you've got that horrid soggy little bag knocking around; what about patenting the idea of grinding the tea leaves so small that they could be made into 'tea pills' that dissolve?

# DAY SIXTEEN

## £327.68 TO £655.36

*Lonely Hearts*

One of the nice things about this job is that sometimes you have the chance to bring a little happiness into the world. Now think about it – what makes people really unhappy? Loneliness. There's a lot of lonely men and women out there just waiting to meet Mr Right and Miss Wonderful (and to get their legs over, of course). Now's your chance to play Cupid and make a few bob into the bargain.

Place this advert in the *Lady*:

**Miss Henrietta Havenstock's Introduction Bureau**

I have a number of wealthy public-school-educated professional gentlemen who are too busy to find the partner they so badly need. Friendship and maybe even marriage could be yours. Twenty guineas and sae brings introductions to clerical, military and professional gentlemen. Total satisfaction or money back. Box 23

Place this advert in *Swedish Big Stuff* (or similar):

**BORED?**

Luscious, lustful, loose housewives want you! Huge list of brazen, busty beauties willing to do anything to anyone anywhere! Just send £5.00 and sae for sample list – satisfaction guaranteed or your money back. Box 13

Simply swap over the names and addresses these two ads bring and cash the cheques, secure in the knowledge that you have promoted just a little human happiness on this otherwise miserable planet.

**Down to Earth**

**DR KARAMAZOV'S** special growing medium for plants. Tailor-made for all bulbs, vegetables or seedlings.

**£25** per packet

**CONTENTS:** earth

# DAY SEVENTEEN

## £655.36 TO £1,310.72

*How to Kidnap the Neighbours' Children*

You may be surprised at the modest target that I set for this project: on the face of it £1,310.72 seems less than one might expect to receive as a reward for the safe return of little Johnny. But experience and parenthood have taught me that parents do not always take the long-term view in these situations. Too many noughts on the ransom and your threat that they will never see the brat again may become tempting.

It is probably a good bet to go for families rich or foolish enough to use fee-paying schools. This is because most such parents are mean and will be reluctant to pay out an entire term's fees and get nothing for it. For the same reason it is best to plan the kidnap early in the term, and preferably in one where Johnny has decided to take woodcarving, canoeing and sky-diving as extras.

As for the actual kidnap, it is not necessary to find a safe house, invest in a fast car or get hold of chloroform to overpower your victim. Why? Because your victim is going to be willing.

This apparently impossible position is attained through the simple recourse of appealing to the child's sense of greed (if he comes from a good, solid middle-class background you can be sure this will have been instilled from an early age). In simple terms you offer to split the reward. However, do be careful to get this in writing, as many modern kids can be unscrupulous. Use the contract I have drawn up below as a guide:

> I, ......., agree to be kidnapped on the ... day of .... for a period of up to a month or until my parents agree to cough up the readies, whichever is the sooner. I also undertake to make pleading phone calls to the said parents at regular intervals begging them to get me safely returned to their loving bosom and fully carpeted Georgian house. For this I will receive the sum of £655.36, to be paid in instalments over the next six months to ensure I do not spill the beans. I understand that during the kidnap period all monies spent on Big Macs, Mars bars, Cokes and any other sundries will be deducted from my share. I enter this agreement in good faith and promise not to sneak.
>
> Signed: ..........

### Paperback Writer

A good way to make money is to write a best seller. *Get Rich Quick* has already earned me well over £1,000,000. But sadly for you that title is taken. However, what about:

'How I helped Les Karamazov become a millionaire'

# DAY EIGHTEEN

## £1,310.72 TO £2,621.44

*Franchising*

There's no doubt about it, franchising is a boom industry. With its positive cash flow it allows great growth for companies to sell anything from socks and knickers to gutters and double glazing. But how do you get into this golden land of opportunity? Certainly not by investing your hard-earned dough in a franchise – that would be too much like hard work. The thing to do is sell franchises to other people.

To start a good franchise you need to be able to point to an already functioning, profitable example of your business. What you need, therefore, is to borrow a multi-million pound enterprise, with low operating costs, no stock to buy up front, room for expansion and that hasn't already been franchised. The answer is of course obvious: the Inland Revenue.

*Just a quick word, if I may.*

The Inland Revenue are always complaining that there is an enormous black economy and that they have nowhere like enough resources to combat this. So today you are going to invest your money in some quarter-page ads in *Exchange and Mart*:

**PART TIME CASH – *FAST***

We all know people on the fiddle – cleaners, plumbers, builders, antique dealers, businessmen, in fact nearly everyone. But do you know how much they really earn? Well now's the chance to find out AND take up to 40% of it!!!

**HOW?**

With our complete Freelance Tax Collector's kit. This is not a joke but a genuine business proposal. With our kit – which includes uniform, identity card, tax tables, and a blue and a red ballpoint pen – you can start TOMORROW!! Simply go up to anyone you know – it might be a member of your family, a neighbour or simply a local tradesman and quiz them about their earnings. With a little practice you will get skilled at persuading them to tell all. Then produce your Independent Guild of Tax Inspectors' card, demand to see their accounts and ask them to hand over 40% of their unearned income.

The cost of this infinitely expandable franchise? Just £2,621.44.

With just one reply you will have doubled your money – in fact you are likely to make much more.

## The Free Lunch

The adage 'there is no such thing as a free lunch' could not be further from the truth – a good 80% of the business community exists entirely on free lunches, not to mention free cars, holidays and villas.

In business, people invite other people out to lunch if they think there is something in it for themselves. This could range from a return, better, lunch, the possibility of some light sexual relief or, most common, a contract to make a great deal of money. This is the area we shall concentrate on.

Dress is of vital importance. Kit yourself out in the most lurid, clashing colours you can find. A yellow shirt with green trousers, white socks and a red jacket would be fine. Now cultivate either an American or Australian accent and, around 11.30 in the morning, drop by some leading estate agents. Very diffidently ask about the possibility of renting 30,000 square metres of prime office space. All but the most somnambulant of agents' eyes will light up. When pressed, explain you are the marketing director of XYZ Inc who are setting up in town next month and that at present you are just taking soundings, visiting a number of agents in the area. At the very mention of rivals you will instantly be invited out to lunch.

This scam can be played out on several successive days, indeed as the rumour gets round that you are on the lookout so the lunches will become more sumptuous – such is the effect of a free market. Once you feel you have exploited the real estate business move on to advertising, PR or some other lucrative area where there is more money and greed than sense.

# DAY NINETEEN

## £2,621.44 TO £5,242.88

*Outward Bound*

For this you will need:

100 sheets of Institute of Motivational Dynamics Analysis notepaper
Six air tickets to Manchester
Five compasses
Five maps of the Brianne Reservoir area, Llandovery, Dyfed
Five packets of Highland shortbread
Five souvenir tartan scarves
Five souvenir toy Loch Ness Monsters
Twenty-five bottles of Laphroaig whisky in carrier bags of five

On Gleneagles Hotel notepaper write to the chairmen and personnel directors of a few dozen target companies mentioning a link-up with the well respected International Institute of Motivational Dynamics Analysis.

Dear ....,
I am pleased to be able to write to you about our new co-operative venture with the International Institute of Motivational Dynamics Analysis.

Together we are offering senior management motivational improvement courses in the Highlands – and as a leading figure in industry we thought you might be interested in sending one of your senior executives on a trial course at no cost, just a contribution to expenses of £1,048.60 (the usual fee is £4,500 per person). Space is limited to five, so this is very much on a first come first served basis. I enclose an agenda for the course.

Yours sincerely,

James MacWhitry

**Agenda**

| | |
|---|---|
| **Day 1:** | Meet at Heathrow Airport<br>9 a.m.<br>Fly to Inverness; in-flight refreshment<br>Arrive hotel; Motivational discussion over coffee<br>Lunch<br>Rest period<br>4.30 p.m.: Orienteering on moor; equipment provided<br>5.30 Informal question and answer session over drinks<br>7.30 Dinner |
| **Day 2:** | 9.30 a.m.: Working breakfast<br>10.30: Lecture: Interpersonal Relationships in Stress<br>10.45: Practical session on grouse moor/salmon river<br>1.30 p.m.: Practical session examining results<br>3.30: Rest period<br>4.00: Five-hour seminar on Interpersonal Relationships |
| **(optional)** | 5.30: Review of day – drinks provided<br>7.30: Working dinner |

*Orienteering starts here.*

Meet your course delegates at Heathrow. Tell them the plane is delayed and hand them a bottle of whisky to be getting on with. It is rather important to this business plan that your customers do not notice that you are getting the nine o'clock shuttle to Manchester instead of the Dan Air flight to Inverness. The Laphroaig should help. During the flight divert attention whenever a pilot's announcement threatens to expose you by singing Scottish folk songs loudly and handing out the shortbread, toys and tartan scarves. Above all, keep topping up the drink. All this will help persuade the delegates that this is a normal educational course. At Manchester bundle your crew into a hire car and drive towards Blackburn.

Once in the middle of the Forest of Bowland push the five executives out, explaining that since the plane was late there has been a change of plan and the Orienteering section has been brought forward. Hand them each a compass and a map of Llandovery, Dyfed, and wish them luck.

I guarantee that you will never hear from your delegates again. Pride, mixed with the excessive alcohol, will prevent them telling the boss they messed up a one-hour stroll in the Highlands and turned it into a two-day hike to Manchester.

# DAY TWENTY

## £5,242.88 TO £10,485.76

*Spreading the News*

Today's plan may seem one of the riskiest – it involves investing all your money in one venture which seems,

**YOU COULD BE A MILLIONAIRE BY THIS TIME NEXT WEEK!**

Yes, it's true. In just seven days I can teach anyone how to be financially independent for the rest of their lives! Twelve months ago I lived in a one-room flat, ate out of tins and worried how I was ever going to support my family. Now, thanks to the X Plan, I have two houses, four cars, a villa abroad and enough money never to have to work again. Incredible? Yes, but you can do it too.

Most people are far too busy working to make any real money. They spend all day slogging their guts out for someone else when they could be earning millions for themselves. I was fortunate enough to stumble across a business plan that enables anyone to turn a few hours' work a week into a huge fortune.

Will I have time to enjoy my wealth? That's virtually all I'll do! I'll have so much time on my hands I'll be able to devote two days a week to helping at least on the surface, to offer very little chance of success. However, with the correct planning it will catapult you in one day from being simply a dabbler to becoming a serious businessman.

Place the following ad in the *Sun*. At current prices you should be able to afford about fifty column centimetres – around a quarter of a page.

charity. By now you will be asking yourself how come I'm willing to give the plan away? The answer is simple – telling other people does not affect it. The more people join in, the better off I am!

**Question:** Does your plan involve selling?
**Answer:** No! There is no selling involved.

**Question:** Do I have to be under a certain age?
**Answer:** Not at all. You can start at any age, from 16 to 80. One of my most successful converts is in her 72nd year!

**Question:** Is it legal?
**Answer:** The X Plan is a legitimate business scheme strictly legal in all countries.

**Question:** How can I take advantage of your plan and start to make BIG money?
**Answer:** Just fill out the form below and send it, along with a cheque for £15.00, to ....., .......,

And remember – if you haven't made your purchase price back in 14 days simply return the book and I will refund your money immediately.

By Tuesday your letterbox will be stuffed with envelopes, each with a fifteen pound cheque. In return you simply send them a copy of this book with the corner of this page turned down. In the unlikely event of someone returning a book refuse to refund their money on the grounds one of the pages is bent.

*Goes like a dream now.*

# DAY TWENTY-ONE

## £10,485.76 TO £20,971.52

*The Karamazov Diet*

It is an interesting observation, I find, that the richer a society the more people pay for food with no nutritional value. Which, in entrepreneurial terms, means more money for less product. The perfect enterprise. In short, slimming is big business.

In order to cash in on this you need to find some large people who have as much money as they do cellulite. This is not difficult. Hang around any department store's food hall, smart restaurant or even up-market wine bar and you will find dozens of them.

As you breeze past, press a leaflet into their pudgy palm:

> Wouldn't you like to lose 16 lbs in a week? In absolute luxury? Guaranteed? You may have tried all the other diets and slimming programs without success – but here's one that is guaranteed to work or your money back. All you have to do is sit back for a week and watch the pounds disappear in one of our super luxury residences. The treatment is not cheap, frankly not everyone will be able to afford our fees of £2,000, but what price can you put on being slim? All we ask is your total commitment and trust – and remember, if you haven't lost at least 16 lbs in your first

week, we will refund all your money AND take you out for an enormous meal.

Phone this number for an immediate appointment

*– every moment lost is another lb put on!*

These may sound impossible claims – they are not. Simply book a very expensive room in one of the best hotels you can find. Bundle your fatty into the hotel and tie it to the bed. Place a bottle of vitamin pills and a carafe of water within easy reach, switch on the TV, leave and lock the door. Return every day to check on your patient's condition, exclaiming, each time you enter: 'Gosh, how slim you look!' They will.

**The Free Snack**

You all know about fun runs, parachute jumps and so on for charity. Well, why not find a deserving charity, a gullible manufacturer and get yourself sponsored for the amount of biscuits you can eat at elevenses or the number of exquisite Belgian truffles at tea.

# DAY TWENTY-TWO

## £20,971.52 TO £41,943.04

*Writing for Profit*

Over the years chain letters have been given a bad name, being associated with bizarre threats and even black magic. Indeed they are now, strictly speaking, illegal.

However, there is still a good deal of mileage in the general principle – namely that each person sends money to the person who sent them the letter before forwarding it to others. There is a way to profit from this idea without breaking the law or entering into the hocus-pocus of traditional chain mail.

Of course the most important part of any such postal scam is the letter itself. After extensive research we at the Institute came up with two possible drafts. The first ran along the lines of 'Pay up or I'll break your legs', which, though surprisingly efficient, does have its drawbacks. The second is printed below:

> Dear ....
> Please find enclosed the details of a very interesting and profitable business venture.
>
> It will take you some time to read through and I urge you to do so when you can fully concentrate as some of the ideas are complex.
>
> This plan really does work. When I first

received a letter similar to this my initial reaction was to throw it straight into the bin. However, out of curiosity I read on and worked out the figures for myself. Frankly, I was impressed. I invested the small amount necessary more as a joke than anything else but was I surprised! Ever since my letterbox has been overflowing with mail – all containing money! My postman is beginning to give me funny looks!

If you follow the instructions carefully you could start making real money too. It's worth a try, believe me!

Yours,
Professor Karamazov Karamazov

*Also enclose the following two sheets:*

## Reports

| | |
|---|---|
| **Report One:** | How to Make a Killing on the Stock Market<br>H. Snoad<br>124 Shakespeare Rd<br>Swindon |
| **Report Two:** | Taking Advantage of Freebies<br>P. Anderson<br>68 Loughborough Avenue<br>Newcastle |
| **Report Three:** | Sources of the Best Mailing Lists |

M. Hending
13 Willesden Park Rd
London SW8

**Report Four:** Multi-level Sales Plans
K. Lamdon
569a Hill Top View
Cardiff

## Instructions

1. Order all four reports listed. Do this by sending £5 and an sae to the name under each report. You must order all four because you will be reselling them.

2. Take the page entitled 'Reports' and replace the first address with your own, dropping the others down so that the last one is removed.

3. Copy the enclosed letter swapping your name for mine.

4. Take the 'Reports' page, letter and instruction sheet to a copy shop and have them copied as many times as you can afford – perhaps start with 200.

5. You can now make up 200 packets similar to the one you received. Mail these out to anyone you can get the address of. You might want to start with friends and relatives, or just pick people out of the phone book.

6. Wait for the money to arrive!

## How It Works

Let's assume you and the people you involve send out 200 packets each (not many, some people may send out more). And let's say that 95% of people who receive them do nothing at all – throw them in the bin. This means 5% take up the challenge and order the reports.

This means that 10 of the people you mail send out their own packs, 200 each. This means 2,000 packets. Of these just 5% follow it up, i.e. 100 responses. Those 100 send out a further 200 each, i.e. 20,000 total. 5% of this is 1,000. The 1,000 send out between them 200,000 and the 5% response on that is 10,000 five-pound notes! Your total income on this, then, is £50 plus £500 plus £5,000 plus £50,000 – a grand total of over £55,000 in cash! And this is assuming that 95% of the people throw your pack straight in the bin. Imagine if the response was better! Start mailing now!

Convincing, isn't it? Furthermore it is not difficult to set up. As you might have guessed, all four names and addresses are really you – simply arrange some accommodation addresses. As for the reports, they are a single sheet of bull, but no-one cares because the whole point is that they are there only to make it seem as if people are buying a product. Used cleverly this scam can generate you a great deal of cash.

## Financial Ecology

This splendid term simply means making the most of under-used assets – and what could be more under-used than a parked car?

Photocopy some flyers with the following irresistible messages:

ALL DAY VALET CAR PARKING SERVICE

If you have ever tried to park your car in the middle of the city, you will be really pleased to know of a new executive service that will pick up your car from the door of your office at 9 a.m., drive it away, look after it all day, and bring it back at 5.30 p.m. ready for you to drive home in. And all for less than it costs at a car park today.

QUARTER PRICE CAR HIRE!!

Incredible but true! We have a limited number of contract cars for hire at a QUARTER of the normal rate. Pick up the car at 9.30 and provided you bring it back by 5.15 we will charge you just one quarter of the usual rate.

## Body Language

As a Karamazov student you will need to adopt many disguises and personas in your pursuit of immense wealth; it is therefore important you become fluent in body language.

Learning to communicate physically is not difficult. Simply study the pictures throughout the book and practise in front of either a mirror or your mother.

## Arise Sir Wayne

It is a little known fact that there is a royal decoration for foreigners known as the Order of the Slipper. It is not often given but is in fact the highest award that the Queen can give to a non-British personage. In the last forty years it has been awarded only as many times. It is generally conferred on naive visiting Americans for services to animals or food (or anything) and it allows the recipient to append the prefix 'The Laudable' to his name. The award is always kept secret till the visitor is in Britain; it is then announced in person by the Privy Chamberlain at the visitor's hotel. Investiture always takes place at night in Westminster Abbey in front of a silent congregation – often unseen in the darkness. Recipients of the Order of the Slipper are expected to attend their investiture in person and may hire their robes (from you; at a cost of some £350.00 – I generally use Barnum's fancy dress hire; Humpty Dumpty usually does, but, when that was already taken, I once used a Captain Hook outfit).

## Fur Storage

It is the custom of the richer fur-coat-owning matrons to keep their furs in good condition by putting them in cold storage for the summer. Although not exactly a growth market, there is probably still a little something to be made by offering this service at a cheap price. You do not even need a fridge since you will keep the furs supple by hiring them out.

# DAY TWENTY-THREE

## £41,943.04 TO £83,886.08

*Becoming a Connoisseur*

Remember Bunker Hunt? That's the way to do it in style – buy the entire world's silver! Corner the market in anything and you can name your price. The trouble is it usually costs rather a lot to corner the market in anything.

There are also a few market conditions that are necessary – you have to be able to buy easily and sell easily. It's not much good trying to corner the market in stuffed alligators or old milk bottles. There must also be a limited supply of whatever you're trying to buy up and people must want it; it's no good buying up all the toilet paper in Bromsgrove for instance – new supplies would soon leak in. Nor is it any good going long on pebbles.

So let's think, what could you do? Cocoa and other crops are traded on various commodity exchanges but it would be rather expensive buying the world's cocoa crop (about three billion pounds). Assuming that you managed to find a rarer commodity which you could monopolise there is always the uncomfortable chance that the world might develop a different taste and then what would you do with, say, seventy million Gloucester black spot pork bellies?

We will have to think laterally. What about the *Financial Times*? A lot of people rely on it, it's fairly easy to buy at source and you've got enough money to buy a day's production. Might be a bit awkward to sell it on though. No, I think we should take heed of that great philosopher Bernie Cornfeld and not 'mess around with lamp globes' but deal in money. That's right – today we are going to corner the market in MONEY!

We are going to corner the market in coins – the humble one penny piece to be precise! These honest little copper discs have a value of – well, by themselves one penny. But like most things they get more expensive the fewer there are. The famous 1933 pennies, when only half a dozen or so were minted, are worth a fortune. So, today you are gradually going to start converting your fortune into pennies. I would suggest the 1982 penny would be a good one since only 100 million were minted (1984 is the next best year with 154 million, and after that 1985 with 200 million). Now a hundred million pennies cost one million pounds – and you haven't quite got that. But as you sift away through the piles of copper don't worry. Quite a number will have been lost and anyway when you have accumulated several hundred thousand the price that a collector pays will start to rise and with a little judicious selling you should make enough profit to get back into the market and buy most of the rest. The advantage of this plan is that it is absolutely safe! Your stock is all in CASH!!

# DAY TWENTY-FOUR

## £83,886.08 TO £167,772.16

*The Art of Making Money*

It is now time to add a bit of class – by taking the Art World for a ride.

1. Line up a third-year art student who can work fast. Talent is not important but accuracy is.

2. Ostentatiously buy a modern painting in an auction. A nice abstract will do.

3. Pass round an expensively bound and tooled 'Registration Book' asking for bidders' names and addresses.

4. Set your art student to work copying the painting.

5. Telephone one of the other bidders and say that the Sultan of Borneo (for whom you were buying) thinks that the painting you have bought offends his religious sensibilities. It is an embarrassing situation and you are willing to sell for the price you bought at.

6. After much haggling settle for 75%.

7. Repeat 5 as many times as possible.

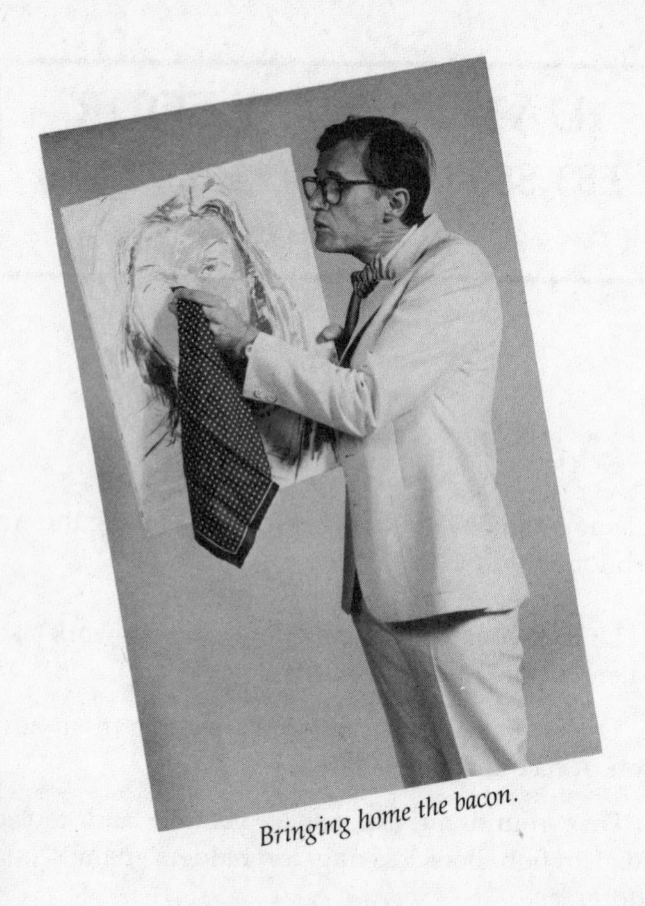

*Bringing home the bacon.*

8. Invite the number one Art Expert to inspect the picture. Anyone may telephone him for his opinion on authenticity.

9. Sell several copies of this masterwork, collect the dosh and disappear.

Note: Even with modern paintings it is important that the paint is dry; an infra-red lamp or hair-dryer usually does the trick.

# DAY TWENTY-FIVE

## £167,772.16 TO £335,544.32

*City Slicker*

ONE HUNDRED AND SIXTY-SEVEN THOUSAND SMACKERS!!! I bet you never thought that you'd get this far! You can now afford to enter the big league of city finance.

1. Ask your stockbroker to get into the Traded Options market with fifty thousand quid's worth of, say, International Sting Ltd. Tell him that you expect the shares to rise and want to capitalise on that.

2. Wait for a fairly dull stock market day – not too much change in prices. Ask another stockbroker to buy fifty thousand quid's worth of the same stock in, say, the name of Murdoch, Rupert.

3. Dress up as a motorcycle messenger, go to the Stock Exchange Announcements Office and file the fact that Murdoch, Rupert and Associates now hold over 5% of the common stock. You might do the decent thing and tell the Panel on Takeovers and Mergers too. You could also tell a few newspapers. In fact the more people that you leak it to the better.

4. The shares will go bananas. The options even more so. Rupert Murdoch is making a bid. You nip round the corner, phone your broker and flog everything.

*Buy! Buy! Buy!*

*Sell! Sell! Sell!*

Technical note: You have to notify the Stock Exchange if you and Persons Acting in Concert own more than 5% of a company; and you have told the gospel truth. It is a fact that you have not yet actually met your Associates but doubtless they would be lovely people if you did. As for Murdoch, Rupert – well that wasn't a comma, it was a bit of dirt on the paper wasn't it?

**The Free Mag**

Need a free copy of a magazine? Call the display advertising department of the mag in question and ask them for a rate card and a current issue.

# DAY TWENTY-SIX

## £335,544.32 TO £671,088.64

*The People of the Golden Coin*

Invent a better mouse-trap and the world will . . . etc. And the same goes for religion. If you can think of a new and better cult, you will have thousands of adoring followers who will bring you presents, pay you tithes, make themselves sexually available to you and so on.

Now what makes a cult better? The answer is of course that it must be outrageously demanding, quite ludicrous in operation, difficult, expensive for the devotee and conspicuously embarrassing.* Try expanding on the following:

> To receive eternal peace on the next level and lasting happiness and tranquillity in this world it is necessary to learn from nature and return from the current frenetic world to a previous era of calm and reason. When you enter the family of the Golden Coin you go back to basics and rediscover the real You. By living in a dog kennel, as all novices do, and giving your wages, antiques, jewellery and any small change to the communal good of the brotherhood, you will find that suddenly many of the worries about the details of everyday life vanish. After receiving instruction

from Father Karamazov for some months, you will, if you are lucky enough, be elevated and received into the first order – the Order of the Duck. Duck people wear plastic bin liners over their clothes and eat only products containing Aspartame and other artificial sweeteners. This is to remind them that the things they previously found sweet in life are only so much rubbish. At this stage, all property owned is also made over to the communal good; at the same time the Duck person may find that any subsidiary worries still remaining about the pressures of society on everyday life also disappear. After one year, the initiate may be learned enough to be received into the Order of the Banana; this order wears only garments made from grey polyester . . . etc., etc.

*Oooooooooommmmmm.*

The only problem with this proposition is thinking up more and harder challenges for your new-found subjects. Who knows, you may find the way of life so enjoyable and profitable that you could retire.

* It should also be based in an impressive country house with lavish arrangements for security – steel perimeters and so forth. This is an invaluable investment for your £335,544.32. You can get very photogenic manor houses in far reaches of Wales and Scotland for a snip. They also have the advantage of being difficult for investigative journalists based in London to get at. The money from your devotees will roll in very quickly – and you could always sell the house on to another cult.

### On Ice

Scene One: A Yuppie about to have a party calls his off-licence to deliver ice. Heavens above – they do not have any! But luckily an ice vending service has left a card. The off-licence calls you, you take the address and the money.

Scene Two: Some three hours later the ice vending service still seems not to have delivered. In a fury the Yuppie opens the door, and lo and behold at his feet is a large plastic bag filled with water. The note with it reads: 'Have knocked and knocked. Bell not working.'

## Hats

The hat may not seem a very important part of your equipment but in fact a hat can say more about a person than virtually anything else. A selection of hats is a vital part of your wardrobe.

Hostility

Amiability

If all else fails . . .

# DAY TWENTY-SEVEN

## £671,088.64 TO £1,342,177.28

*Making a Killing*

You have now reached a critical stage in the Karamazov Method. It is your last day and you have already made your penny into £671,088.64. It is a dangerous time. You feel confident, you feel proud and above all you feel rich. You are tempted to reward yourself with a little present – a small Ferrari runabout or perhaps a Chelsea mews. However, if you start spending money now you will never become the millionaire you should be. Stick to the plan, keep doubling your money – in just one more day you can spend all you like.

### Making a Killing on the Property Market

The secret of the property business is to find a depressed, unpopular, run-down area, buy up as many houses as possible and then convince buyers that it is a dynamic, fashionable, up-and-coming 'village' which they must move to immediately. This usually involves keeping your ear to the ground, going to auctions and dressing in suits from Burtons. It can also take some time to make your fortune – anything up to six months. You have just a day and so must take some short cuts. How? The answer is deceptively simple. Natural disasters.

# How to Make Natural Disasters Work for You

It is a proven fact that natural disasters lower the price of houses dramatically. After the great San Francisco earthquake of 1921 you could have bought up most of the Bay for the price of a bus ticket back east. However, what people do not realise is that the mere threat or possibility of a disaster can have an equally dramatic effect on prices.

All you need to do is persuade people that some catastrophic event is about to happen. It is not necessary to persuade a whole town, just a few well-chosen individuals will do. They will thank you, see you as their saviour and, congratulating themselves on their foresight, sell up and move out. Other people will notice. They'll get nervous and sell too. Soon panic will set in and people will be desperate to get rid of their houses for virtually anything. This is where you step in and, with a show of charity, take the houses off their hands for a few hundred pounds each.

Once you have invested your £671,088.64 you can let it be known that the threat of catastrophe is over. People will want their houses back, the place will become desirable once more and – of course – prices will go up. You then simply sell the properties back to their original owners for several times what you paid for them.

## Choosing Your Disaster

There are an almost infinite number of disasters to choose, from avalanches to whirlwinds. However, don't get carried away – not all disasters are equally credible. People are less likely to believe a tidal wave is about to hit Croydon than they are Brighton. Below are some suggestions and possible locations:

| | |
|---|---|
| Avalanche | Inverness (though nobody really wants to live there anyway) |
| Drought | Maidstone |
| Earthquake | Bath |
| Floods | London |
| Geothermic ruptures | Hayling Island |
| Hurricanes | Anywhere in the South East |
| Ice age | Scunthorpe (this is a tricky one) |
| Locusts | Leeds |
| Meteor | Kirby |
| Plague | Chichester |
| Rains | York |
| Tornado | Manchester |
| Waterspout | Southampton |

## Spreading the Rumour

No matter how good your disaster, it will come to nothing unless you can convince other people it is imminent. It is no good simply wearing a sandwich board declaring the end of the world – you must be at once dramatic yet convincing, frightening yet credible. This is where some simple PR techniques will come in handy.

The first rule of PR is that journalists will believe anything if it satisfies two criteria:

1. The story seems incredible.
2. They think they have an exclusive.

Add to this a certain reluctance to give the information and you are guaranteed major coverage.

Here is the plan of action:

1. Decide on disaster – say a tidal wave to hit Eastbourne.

2. Telephone a leading meteorological expert and ask him if it is totally impossible for a tidal wave to hit Eastbourne – he will undoubtedly say it is not quite impossible.

3. Telephone all the leading estate agents in the area and ask if it is true that house prices are falling. When they say no, tell them that all the other agents said they were.

4. Telephone a journalist and say there is some scandal about house prices falling – be mysterious.

5. Telephone the same journalist in a different voice complaining that information has been leaked from the Met Office and pointing out that they cannot print confidential information.

6. Telephone the journalist once more, again leaking the information about a tidal wave.

The journalist will now think he's onto the best story of his life. He'll call round the estate agents, seek legal advice and by the evening have a major story on the impending tidal wave. He may even sell his house.

Once the rumour is under way all you need do is buy up the properties as they come on the market. It is important at this point to appear very stupid – people love to think they are pulling a fast one on an idiot. You must seem totally ignorant of the news of doom.

**Why Didn't I Think of That?**

I don't know about you but I'm always losing my ball-point pens. And if you look at how they are made, it does seem unnecessary to put that outer bit of plastic on. Imagine a long tube, filled with ink, that tapered off to a string so that you could tie it to things.

# Conclusion

The impossible has become true: you are a millionaire, in fact you are rather more than a millionaire, by almost a third. The extra will come in handy to pay taxes, grease a few palms and buy something nice for dinner.

## *What Next?*

Having achieved your aim and become stinking, obscenely rich you may feel that life has no more challenges for you. Do not despair. Now that you do not have to spend time on such humdrum matters as forging a bus pass or working out how to eat off six pounds a week, you can afford to allow your mind to concentrate on Higher Things. In case you are wondering what these are, here are some suggestions:

The Future of Mankind

Art, Morality and Particle Physics

Why Bits of Skin by your nail are so tempting to tear off with your teeth.

However, judging by past students it is unlikely that you will want to spend much more than twenty minutes contemplating such things. Fortunately I have compiled a series of guides that will give you new goals in life. All are available in plain brown paper wrapping from the publisher:

How to Get a Knighthood
How to Get Interviewed on TV
How to Get Everyone to Admire You
How to Live a Very Long Time

Of course the true entrepreneur can never be happy unless he or she is making money. You will not be satisfied with a mere million but will see this as just the start of a promising career as a multi-millionaire. To satisfy this need I have recently completed a companion volume, entitled *Get Even Richer, Even Quicker*. This is the outcome of years of research and is a comprehensive guide to getting REALLY REALLY rich. As you might expect, such advice does not come cheap, but I think you will agree that it is well worth the cover price of £1,342,177.28.

*All legal correspondence and enquiries concerning the contents of this book should be forwarded to: PO box 74, Tangiers.*